About the Author

R. A. Boyd is a registered nurse with thirty years of experience in various fields of medicine.

Diary of a Nobody... Musings and Prose of an Emergency Nurse

R. A. Boyd

Diary of a Nobody... Musings and Prose of an Emergency Nurse

Olympia Publishers
London

wwww.olympiapublishers.com
OLYMPIA PAPERBACK EDITION

Copyright © R. A. Boyd 2023

The right of R. A. Boyd to be identified as author of
this work has been asserted in accordance with sections 77 and 78 of
the Copyright, Designs and Patents Act 1988.

All Rights Reserved

No reproduction, copy or transmission of this publication
may be made without written permission.
No paragraph of this publication may be reproduced,
copied or transmitted save with the written permission of the publisher,
or in accordance with the provisions
of the Copyright Act 1956 (as amended).

Any person who commits any unauthorized act in relation to
this publication may be liable to criminal
prosecution and civil claims for damage.

A CIP catalogue record for this title is
available from the British Library.

ISBN: 978-1-80439-179-2

This is a work of fiction.
Names, characters, places and incidents originate from the writer's
imagination. Any resemblance to actual persons, living or dead, is
purely coincidental.

First Published in 2023

Olympia Publishers
Tallis House
2 Tallis Street
London
EC4Y 0AB

Printed in Great Britain

Dedication

To my most amazing boys.

The Response

A daughter to her father:
Dad, I'm going to nursing school.

The response:
Why would you do that? A nurse is just a glorified hand maid.

A Nurse to her husband:
Today was exhausting. I really need to decompress.

The response:
All you nurses complain. What makes you think your job is tough?

A divorced Nurse to her firefighter boyfriend:
It would be nice for nurses to have substantial benefits.

The response:

It's not my problem you stood in the wrong line.

A Nurse to her patient:
I'm here with the ultrasound to get your IV started.

The response:
I think you nurses are overpaid. There's nothing special about you.

A Nurse to her leadership:
We need to ensure staff has appropriate PPE for the novel virus.

The response:
We don't have the budget; keep working and be happy you have a job.

A daughter to her deceased father:
Dad, you were right.

This is but a Reflection

It is my review and telling of a singular journey, my journey. It is a collection of story and prose of desiring, and becoming, an "emergency nurse."

As fate would have it, this is written, heavy-hearted, with arduous years behind me, as I have had to make the decision to leave the Emergency department after twenty-plus years. The decision to leave was, and is still, painful.

Emergency medicine is a calling. It is something so deeply engrained into one's being, that to step away, although saving one's own sanity, is almost a regrettable decision.

I have no illusions with regard to the fact that I am not set apart from anyone else who has had to come through hard times, or has had to make difficult decisions. I am ever grateful for my experiences and opportunities. I have learned much about myself, human nature, society, the value of life, and God.

I say that I am not set apart from anyone else because I, too, could easily be the "nobody" you pass on the street every day. The Emergency department has a way of making it very clear to those that work within its halls that we all could easily be one bad decision away from the homeless beggar on the street corner, or the drug addict, or those suffering and possibly succumbing to a loss, or the thousands of others who let the pressure of life weigh them down.

Why do I say this? How do I know this? Because... I am, and have been, witness to others' self-destructive behaviors; behaviors that we are all capable of enacting. Some make the decision to act and to hell with the consequences; others temper their actions and attempt, sometimes feebly, to navigate away from action that would lead them astray or cause further damage.

Years of working in the Emergency department brings to light a sharp awareness that we all have a tipping point. We just don't know what that point is until it is breached.

It is in how we interact with ourselves and others, how we perceive events and our environment, that has the effect of weaving our life's tapestry. We have the ability to make it bright and colorful. We have the ability to make it drab and coarse. It takes but one loose stitch, one loose end, to be pulled for the entirety of our lives to become unraveled. In that, that is where a dissembling can happen.

Observe

Do you see the high tide rolling in?
Look at the waves,
Rumbling, crushing,
The sound so loud that you can't
think, only observe.

Do you see the tide rolling out?
Look at the waves carry away,
Wiping away the castles that were
built,

The knowing that it swept away time and hard work,
You can't stop it, only observe.

Do you see the clouds moving in?
Look at the rain falling,
Steady, rhythmic,
Increasing in intensity, you are powerless, able to only observe.

Do you see the clouds darkening, ominous?
Look at the rain turning into rivers,
Flooding,
The knowing that it powers over, taking anything in its path,
You can't stop it, only observe.

The tides, the waves, the clouds, the rain, the floods,
They have the potential to be devastating, but are out of man's control.

The anger, the sadness, the drugs, the alcohol, the self-mutilation,
These have the potential to be devastating, but are under man's

control. Yet man chooses to act as if there is no control.

So the tides of anger, the waves of sadness, the clouds of drugs, the reign of alcohol, the flood of self-mutilation continue…
…and I can't stop it, I can only observe.

And it is within the walls of the Emergency department that one can also find a unique way of humbling your character. Within that humbling, one can build internal monuments; capturing the glory of your life and the life of those around you. This weaving, this humbling, this building, propels one further into the desire to help others who seek solace and comfort, regardless of the risks one might suffer to one's own well-being.

Emergency medicine is a co-mingling of all extremes of the human form. One must have a level of accepting, coupled with a unique ability to working within, an insane, sometimes perverse, reality.

There is not a lot of "normalcy" in what happens within the halls of an Emergency department, this I can assure you.

So the question becomes, why does anyone come to be, and stay, in Emergency medicine?

That is not a rhetorical question. It is also not a hollow question. It is a question meant to expand one's observation in attempts to examine, dissect, and actively interpret those who have the tenacity to continue showing up day after day. To ask, "What is their driving force?"

My calling came to me while watching, on television, a devastating plane crash in a remote area of New York many, many years ago. I remember thinking to myself, *I could do that. I could help those people.*

That singular thought began my journey into the world of medicine, specifically, into the world of nursing. I started my professional career on a medical-surgical unit, advancing to critical care, until I found myself in the demanding world of the Emergency department.

There are many facets of medicine, of nursing. As students are exposed to the variety, and levels, of care that is necessary to see a patient, and family, through an illness or medical process, they begin to shape their path forward. Students gravitate to their passion, their desired level of investment, their interest.

It takes a unique set of physical, mental, emotional, educational, behavioral, and personal skills to choose, and then remain, in an Emergency department.

Unanswered

Depression. Anger. Sadness. Despair.

Descriptors of what can break a soul down
Bring even the strong to their knees
Haunt their days
Cloud their judgement

Questions reflecting

Used as a mirror
A snapshot of the soul

Questions asked
Used to draw out behaviors
Identify emotions

Have you experienced a recent loss?
Have you experienced a recent lack of
a social support system?
Do you feel depressed?
Do you feel hopeless?

Questions lingering
Hung heavy in the air
Unanswered, but not by the patient

I have heard it said often enough that working in the Emergency department is akin to being in an abusive relationship. It is a cycle of hope and devastation.

The hope exists that maybe today, maybe today will be the day of difference, of finally bringing and subduing violence and chaos into kindness and calm. The weary eyes, the half-smile, the drooped shoulders, the sore feet and the knowing that tomorrow will come and call upon the Emergency Department to be ever at the ready.

And when tomorrow comes, it will bring with it deep demands, dysfunction, disease, death, and many unknowns. But those in the Emergency department stand stalwart and true; they will face tomorrow head on.

Court Jester

Court Jester.
Working the court for platitudes and baubles.
Tricks to entertain… skill honed thru the years.
Quick, light, adept; plying the crowd.
Keep the balance, be immune from disparaging yawps.

Many faces, young and old.
Eyes burning through my soul, searching for a moment of…
Hope? Happiness? Relief? An antidote to a misery?

Emergency Nurse.
Emblem lunchbox and pizza, a leadership dust off "atta boy."
Short supplies, no lunch breaks… skills honed thru brutal hours.
Quick, light, adept; flexing to meet numbers and metrics.
Keep the balance, bend, but do not break.

Many faces, young and old.

Bloodied bodies burned into my mind.
Soul-wrenching wails echo in my ears.
Eyes burning through my soul, searching for a moment of...
Hope? Happiness? Relief? An antidote to a misery?

I am the Court Jester. I am the Emergency Nurse

Returning to the question 'why does anyone come to be, and stay, in an Emergency Department?' The answer is far deeper than phrases such as, "to do good," or, "to save lives." Responding in this vein, with such rote phrases, equates to shallow and disconnected answers, or possibly, a lack of comprehension regarding the importance of the Emergency Department.

For example, I would argue that it is reasonable, and appropriate, to apply those rote responses to every extension and facet of medicine and nursing. Those responses could encompass any medical or nursing intervention from birth through death, from an inpatient to an outpatient setting, from rural to urban care, and the list goes on. So, those rote answers do not capture the essence of the Emergency department. Those rote answers can equally apply to the ancillary departments that support every aspect of medicine and patient care. The hospital's ancillary departments are framed, built, and are in existence for the purpose of "doing good" and providing necessary adjuncts to "save lives." All ancillary departments are truly valuable in the role they serve in assisting patient and family care, and ultimately, human health.

Therefore, in providing such rote answers, one has not identified the significance of Emergency medicine. One has not identified what sets Emergency medicine apart from all else in medicine or healthcare. All that is left is a sad reality that there is still a true lack of comprehension, of the function and purpose of the Emergency department, in society.

To highlight that point, I provide an example of a very one-sided conversation I had once with a spinal surgeon. He offered his unsolicited perspective on Emergency Department physicians as follows, "ER docs are useless. They know a little about a lot, but don't know a lot about anything."

The pomp and arrogance with which he hurled this statement reflected his inability to understand the importance of Emergency medicine. I believe that it would have been a futile attempt to disabuse him of his lack of comprehension, so I smiled and walked away.

Rushed orchestra

Who is the triage nurse rushing back? A child?

This is not good. Everybody knows the rushed carry, the hurried movements, the lines of concern on his face foreshadows the worst.

Limp. No color. Does the child have a pulse?

Chest compressions. Intubation. IVs. Medications. An organized, frenzy orchestra moves around the child.

Limp. No color. No pulse.

Aggressive efforts continue. "Amazing Grace" is heard softly, singing.

A mother. Holding her child's hand, prays for mercy as she sings.

Limp. No color. No pulse.

The ED physician holds the grieving mother. Attempt to console a loss of such great magnitude is an impossible task.

Privacy. The last intimate moment of a mother with her child.

The physician looks directly at me, lost, distraught. I hug her, tight.

She sobs on my shoulder. I attempt to console her. She gave her all to save a child's life.

Weary. Exhausted. The day is not done.

Look. Down the hall.

Who is the triage nurse rushing back?

I postulate that a spinal surgeon is a singular entity. He is a surgeon who specializes, yes; but he is someone who functions within his own silo and cannot reach beyond his specialty.

Understandably, there is a purpose for his working within a silo. Any patient would want a spinal surgeon to have mastered his specialty. Any patient would want to have a surgeon who possesses an immense knowledge of, and is laser-focused on, the procedures and necessary surgical interventions to a spinal malady.

But, the surgeon has little understanding of the many varied and intricate human facets that must work cohesively, to maintain a life. The surgeon has a general sense of those facets, but has slowly replaced that knowledge in exchange for his skill and mastery of his profession.

The responsibility of the cohesive inner workings of the human form will fall to the hospitalist, or intensivist, to manage. It is that same responsibility that has also fallen to the "useless ER docs," well before any other physician is called to participate in the patient's care.

I will never take away the years he put into medical school, residency, and practice; those years have served him well and he should be respected for that. I will acknowledge that he has great knowledge of his specialty and how to potentially approach, and potentially fix, a very singular problem; he should be respected for that also. I will argue that that knowledge doesn't always translate into success. The surgeon has a pocket of excuses if the surgery isn't successful; and can easily turn the lack of success on the faulty equipment he was forced to work with: the patient themselves.

Well? Weren't you already broken when you came to see the surgeon? What did you expect? A surgeon can only work with what you, the patient, provide as a canvas for his work of surgical art. He cannot guarantee the outcome nor does he intend to manage the entirety of the human form.

I assume that this is where some might take offense to my very direct assessment. My assessment does not, in any way, diminish the surgeon's intervention, skill, or expertise. The surgeon offers hope, and the potential of a better future, for his patients, through his specialized practice and intervention.

My assessment is just very real, direct, and truthful; and I have seen it a thousand times play out. The promise of relief from pain, or disability, or ailment gets broken… the original canvas was in disrepair prior to the surgeon's intervention, and unfortunately, remains in a state of disrepair after.

I am just a realist, and not afraid to state the obvious. If the obvious insults your delicate sensibilities, then you may want to stop reading. Feigning insult, in the face of a reality, serves no purpose.

A very real practice that does serve a purpose is first to hold up a mirror to yourself and ask forgiveness from others. Why do I say this? I say this knowing that each person has once mumbled something similar to the spinal surgeon's barb. I say this knowing that each person has thrown an unsubstantiated insult at someone else at some time. I say this knowing that each person has perpetrated acts of being less-than-perfect upon someone at some time. I say this knowing that apathy exists.

<u>*Please stop*</u>

Please stop.
Please do not call me a "hero" now.
Where were your words of praise 10, 20, 30 years ago during decades of varied health crisis?

Your fear.
Your fear of disease provided you an opportunity to see me.
Who do you think worked the front lines of H1N1, Swine Flu, HIV, Hepatitis, Ebola, Measles, and Tuberculosis outbreaks?

I am the same person.
I am the same person who gave selflessly then as I do now.

Will you continue to show me the same respect?
The respect you feign today, only coming forward in light of your own personal fear, will it be there 10 years from now?
Or will you forget my sacrifice as your fear recedes?

Only time will tell.
Time will tell who you are.
Are you stalwart and true? Or are you feigned and fake?

Maybe you once had acted in arrogance and pomp, believing that you, somehow, sit above another, like the spinal surgeon. If so, then in essence, you have forgotten that we all began and exist as simple human beings. We are tasked with never forgetting that fact or we lose real truth and perspective.

These acts may not have been grave or severe. These acts do not have to be grave or severe. But do you really know their ultimate end power that was exerted? No, you do not.

Maybe you were that person who has looked down upon others? Maybe you once called another human being "useless" or "non-essential?" Believing your station in life was elevated by title, money, family, education, or whatever lie you told yourself. And it was a lie.

Maybe you were that parent who just shoved a cell phone at your child to keep them quiet? Choosing not to listen to, or engage with, your child. If you would have chosen instead to engage your child, you would have taught them love, patience, and acceptance.

Maybe you were that person who believed themselves to be quick-witted and tossed around sarcasm and gross humor? Imagine if your words left physical marks that you could see, instead of the deep wounds of internalized public humiliation and shame.

Maybe you were that person? I am sure you were, at least once.

I point this human defect out to assure you that the one place in a hospital that does not feign insult, take offense, dawdle in ridiculous ego petting, or forget that we are all just human, is the Emergency department.

The Emergency department is a place of true equal treatment of the human form. Prioritizing care based on the emergency presented. The Emergency department offers every possible type of care and intervention equally to all. There is no "cutting to the front of the line." Care is non-judgmental and based solely on someone presenting with a dire and true emergency. It is that simple.

Yet, the Emergency department and its cohesive team, the team that works steadfastly to treat all medical conditions, have been the recipients of undeserved accusations and misplaced frustrations. These accusations and frustrations stem from misguided and misconstrued personal perception. The personal perception of what one believes to be a critical event; not what is factually considered a critical event.

Yes

Yes? May I assist you?
(I ease my breath and steady my
hand as I press the toggle to shut off the
call light.)

Yes. I apologize. I'm sorry that I wasn't
able to come sooner.
(I offer you a smile, but I know that
the brightness is not yet back in my eyes.
Can you not smell the death that clings
onto my clothes?)

Yes. I understand. You have been
waiting for a pillow.
(Did you not see staff members
hustling by your room responding to the
trauma call?)

Let me offer you that pillow now.
(Do you not see how luck has you in
its favor today? You will live to see
tomorrow.)

Yes. I know you have been waiting to
see the doctor for some time now. Yes. I

understand. I know that your time is valuable also.
(We had to crack open his chest. Every drop of blood, spilling from his chest, thundered as it hit the trauma bay floor. How did you not hear that?)

Is there anything more that I can do for you as you wait?
(Do you not hear the sobbing? Do you not understand?)

Yes. I will dim your lights.
(And I will pray for you. For your selfishness, your lack of wanting to understand, that, maybe, just one other person IS more important than you today.)

If you have never walked down the hallways of an Emergency department, agenda-free, except to bear witness to the calamity, the controlled chaos, you are naive. And be very thankful for that naivety. To be witness to true human suffering, social discord, dismemberment, death, life, and time lost, takes its toll. No one is immune. They may be quiet, just as a mime acts, as they suffer in agonizing silence, or they demonstrate their suffering in behaviors, like a late-night drink, one too many.

The journey into Emergency medicine is laced with doubt, feigned mastery in emotional control, emptiness, and questions. It is also laced with anonymity, great happiness, watching the light in the room change with each soul that passes, and a greater awareness of just how precious time is.

We are the strength, bond, and pivotal link in the chain in your survival, but so easily forgotten. (Or "useless," as the spinal surgeon portends.) The critical time spent within the Emergency department is overshadowed by the days spent in another part of the hospital during your healing process.

<u>The last call</u>

The last call of today's shift.
A paramedic reports "CPR in progress."
Assemble the team.
Coordinate the plan.
Synchrony becomes life.

A siren moves closer.
Flashing lights signal the urgency.
Heartrates increase.
Energy thrums with intensity.

A patient breaches the doors.
No pulse, no signs of life.
The practiced dance
of medical intervention,
Seconds turn into minutes,
minutes into an hour.

A sober quiet falls over the room.
Death, today, the victor.
All present slowly depart, heads hung,
Defeated.

A sound of someone weeping can be heard.
Starts as a faint sobbing,
filled with raw emotion,
heaviness of the soul.
I glance around.
Cars surround me driving in the lanes, the trees are rushing by. That someone is me,
Hands on the wheel,
tears coursing down my cheeks, alone, after that last call.

All this might sound like I am disgruntled, angry; a mad old badger. Actually, it is quite the contrary.

I am grounded in my faith of Christ. I know that He is the Creator and I am but His servant, called to His work. I know that I am guided by His edict. I am here to serve, to listen, to intervene, and to be available when another asks. I know that control is not mine; it is but a perception, or rather a lie, if we are going to be honest.

I have also learned to be cautious of people, as I have seen humanity in decline. I am forced to work within a framework that I no longer understand. I must continually provide the utmost in care and respect, but yet, not deserving the same in return.

Who would continue to work in such an environment except out of duty to a Greater Power? Who would continue to work in such an environment except out of duty to a higher calling? Who would continue to work in such an environment, compelled to extend to another, disregarding their own safety, except out of knowing that giving of oneself is morally right?

Many years ago, I had the honor of having had a conversation with a military veteran. He had honorably served in the marines during the early part of the Afghanistan war.

He was currently working as an assistant coach with my son's basketball team. Whenever possible, I would go to the practice and just be present.

We had gotten to talking, just random small talk. Our conversation led to my asking about his background and how he came into being the team's assistant coach. The conversation eventually led him to inquire about my employment, as not many moms came to just stand against the wall and observe basketball practice.

What came next was humbling.

This former marine, who saw combat, thanked me for my continued service in the Emergency Department. He said that he couldn't imagine what it must be like, day after day, year after year, to continue to show up and do the job.

He said that although, yes, combat was hard, he knew that it would be short-lived and he would be able to have a reprieve. But the Emergency department? This marine equated it to a continual, no-end-in-sight, combat zone.

Witness

Why are you screaming?
Why must you continue to flail your arms and legs?
Why did you just spit at me?

What makes you think I should tolerate your vile obscenities?
What gives you a right to punch at me?
What reaction are you expecting when you hurl possibly infectious bodily fluid my way?

When did you put aside manners?
When can you justify violence against a person who has done you no harm?
When did polite courtesy escape your being?

Have you ever thought that your words write your pages of life?
Have you given consideration that each body is a temple of God?
Have you lost the ability to conceptualize grace?

Who will be your ultimate judge?
Who will forgive your unwarranted anger?
Who will hold you accountable?

Rest assured it will not be me. I am but God's servant, here to act with humility, honor, patience, neutrality, understanding, and in His Grace. I will continue my duty to my fellow human being, regardless of the indignities thrown my way, or the threats against my person. I look for no reward, I but seek His Grace.

I will stand in faith…
… I will stand here as witness as you continue…

Please remember that at no point in time did any staff member in an Emergency department come to your place of residence and forcibly bring you into the department. But yet, we are treated as if we violated your person, and are forcibly detaining you. YOU came to us. I will let you know that the same door you entered in swings the other way to let you out, trust me.

In that same vein, prior to allowing your hasty exit from our care, I will let you know that we will do everything possible to try to make you comprehend, and hopefully accept, the need to allow us to continue our work for your health. Let us help you help yourself, find a solution, or refer you to other necessary resources. Our goal is your health, nothing more, nothing less.

Oh, there are the pundits and politicians who pick and choose what we, as a society, should be rejoicing, but that is a means to their end, their agenda, their narrative. Those are the people who throw out judgements and criticism in attempts to manipulate society, like the circus ringleader orchestrating the show, deftly plying and shifting your attentions.

Turnstile commuters

Have you ever had to look into a patient's eyes as they ask you to "tell my wife I love her" before they go pulseless?
This I wonder as you attempt to boost morale with "free donuts and coffee" as I enter the hospital's main entrance.

When did you last juggle how to prioritize a patient's life, limb, medication, or treatment while caring for 7, 8, or 9 patients?
This I wonder as you short staff our department... again.

How many times have you missed a Christmas feast, holiday celebration, or family gathering?

This I wonder as you "balance" the schedule without any consideration for those who perform acts of immense humanity as they miss, once again, their family and friends.

What have you sacrificed recently? This I wonder as you ration personal protective equipment and advise the staff that overtime "is being considered," maybe, a possibility next pay period.

Leadership... It must be an interesting job... to hold a title, or an office, or a useless degree that hangs on your wall... to do little to nothing to improve the actual quality of another person's life... to be able to say "I'm part of the leadership team," yet have no true leadership ability in the midst of battle, life crisis, true chaos... to lack accountability, yet hold everyone else accountable.

One day, you may see yourselves as you are seen by those of us who do the real work... as an emptiness, void of true empathy and human understanding... as an obstacle, void of the knowledge necessary to enact worthy decisions... as nothing more than a commuter passing thru the turnstile... because you will pass thru these halls, briefcase in hand, and never be remembered nor missed.

    I pull in the pundits and politicians because they bring noise and confusion. They pull society away from deep introspection and the personal conversations that should only be had between patient and healthcare provider. They try to insert themselves in places where they shouldn't belong. For example, how can any society utilize all available resources in attempts to maintain a non-viable human form on life support, and at the same time not provide quality resources, pushing to abort a true and viable life? Do you see the oxymoron?

    If humans are given life by our Creator and to Him we return, then why are we not allowing for those we love to enter His Kingdom? By human-admitted and selfish desires, we deny those we love the freedom from being unshackled from this existence. But yet, when He gives life, there are those that would choose to deny that life.

    In that alone, there is no harmony, there is only confusion. And in that confusion, comes anger and discord among people. And from the unrest among people is born a decline in humanity, a need to be cautious, to thoughtfully examine ourselves and the world around us.

Blind

Young lives.
Old lives.
Unborn lives.
Black lives.
Blue lives.
White lives.
Red lives.
Military lives.
Poor lives.
Rich lives.
Religious lives.
Secular lives.
Drug lives.
Athletic lives.
Single lives.
Married lives.
They ALL matter.
There is NO difference.
If you see a difference…
…then you are blind.

I have seen medicine, and its character, change dramatically over my years. Change is inevitable and part of the life process, medicine included, but what I have witnessed has been a tsunami of what I perceive as ethics breach.

I have observed a significant shift, that has traversed many lines, and, honestly, gives me trepidation. As I walk the halls AWAY from the Emergency department, to hear physicians, surgeons, nurses, and others, be they ancillary staff or visitors or patients, participate in dialog that actively seeks to segregate people on their "vaccination status," or even worse, whisper that death is their due, is a harbinger for dark days to come.

In all my years, I have never encountered any medical professional, or ancillary staff member, express such divisive remarks. Nor in all my years, did I ever see medicine stop working, scheduling, performing, or intervening on account that a human might have a communicable disease. We had just rolled up our proverbial sleeves and continued to get to work, healing one patient at a time, never fearing, never running away from who or what was presenting.

Hero to zero

Hero to zero...

I showed up.
I held your hand.

I comforted you.
I cared for you.

Hero to zero…

PPE was scarce.
"Reuse it until the integrity is compromised," they said.
Patient assignments exceeding a single nurse's ability
No reprieve from human loss or suffering.
Swimming in a pool of infectious diseases, COVID now added in.

Hero to zero…

Now you say I have no choice.
Now you say I am a murderer if I chose what's right for my body.
Now you say I should be denied care, or insurance, if I get sick.
Now you say I am inadequate to maintain my position.
Now you say that I should be ashamed of myself.

Hero to zero…

I was never really your hero was I?
I was just a pawn, a puppet, to parade
in front of the hospital.
Easily tossed away once the show is
over and the applause faded.

I no longer serve your purpose if I
don't prostrate myself before you.
I am now your zero.
Expendable.
Hero to zero...

As I have said before, this is a singular view, my view.

I will tell you this... everyone's best chance at life exists in the Emergency Department. We never stopped. We never ran away. We never argued about what patient we will and won't take. The Emergency Department take them ALL. Regardless of race, religion, gender, vaccination status, political views, socioeconomic status, we take them ALL. Day or night, holiday or weekend, old or young, new disease or known disease, we never stop.

We care for everyone without a second thought, hesitation, or bias.

We are the true front line. We are the ones who step up and step in when others would hesitate or close their doors. Our commitment to our patients is far deeper and more unbreakable than we are ever given credit for.

We never close our doors.

We accept you in however you present to us.

We fight for you when others give up.

We are your true angels here on Earth.

I am the "nobody" that intervenes in your life when you need it, at the most crucial moment... I am an Emergency nurse.